SAND·tiquity

ARCHITECTURAL MARVELS
YOU CAN BUILD AT THE BEACH

SAND·*tiquity*

BY

MALCOLM WELLS
KAPPY WELLS
CONNIE SIMÓ

WILLOW CREEK PRESS

MINOCQUA, WISCONSIN

Published by Willow Creek Press
P.O. Box 147
Minocqua, Wisconsin 54548

Designed by Deb Claus

For information on other Willow Creek titles,
call 1-800-850-9453

Library of Congress Cataloging-in-Publication Data

Wells, Malcolm.
  Sandtiquity / by Malcolm Wells, Kappy Wells, Connie Simó. -- [2nd ed.]
   p. cm.
Prev. ed. published: New York : Taplinger Pub. Co., 1980.
Simó's name appears first on the earlier edition.
ISBN 1-57223-094-0
1. Sand craft. 2. Sandcastles. 3. Sand sculpture. I. Wells, Kappy. II. Simó,
Connie. III. Title.
TT865.S55 1999
736' .9--dc21   99-18769
             CIP

Printed in Canada

CONTENTS

INTRODUCTION

Twenty years have passed since we produced the first edition of *Sandtiquity*. In those days, Jimmy Carter was President, the Cold War was hot, and you may not even have been born. A lot has happened in the last two decades, but the beach and the ocean seem as timeless as ever.

Going back to Nauset Beach on Cape Cod, to build the new sandtiquities and to take new photos was, for us, like being twenty years younger. It was a nice experience for us and one we hope this book will give you. But you'll have to be careful. As more about the dark side of sunlight is known, dermatologists advise much shorter exposures to ultraviolet rays and using plenty of sunblock. We tried to follow the new rules carefully. Occasionally, though, we were so absorbed in our work that we forgot, and that reminded us to remind you that the projects in this book are so much fun, and so rewarding, it will take a conscious effort to avoid sunburn. *Don't forget!*

Another change from our 1978 procedures was that of using a better tool. You can easily do every one of these buildings using only a straight edge, such as a shingle or piece of beach fence, but unless you're careful, your fingertips will leave little telltale indentations in the sandy surfaces.

That's why we added a rib to the back of the flat stick. With all the sand-packing involved, this change has saved us many hours and it can do the same for you. But remember: the good ol' flat stick has been used with great success by thousands of our readers.

Try to find a beach where the sand isn't coarse and pebbly. fine damp sand packs hard in seconds and cuts like cream cheese. That's when sandtiquity is at its best, a seaside delight. You'll do such nice work, you'll want to take pictures of your masterpieces, before the tide sweeps them away. Two suggestions will help you take good pictures:

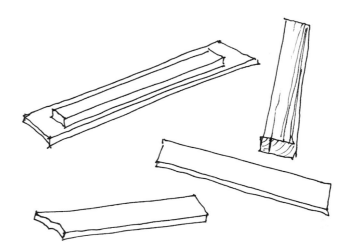

1) *Shoot toward the light–dark corner of each solid. This will reveal the solidity of the form.*
2) *Get your chin into the sand and make your structures tower above you.*

Okay. Enough words. On to the beach!

Connie, Mac & Kappy

The only tools we needed were a straight, flat stick of wood and our eager hands. The damp sand did the rest, holding an extraordinary variety of shapes and angles. Some passersby insisted we must have used cardboard inserts to give us such crisp, solid-looking edges, but we claimed that the structures were buried there — we had simply brushed away the sand.

1

BEFORE YOU BEGIN

The straight edges we used at first were always found things — a piece of broken dune fencing, a scrap of shingle, anything that had a flat side for tamping surfaces and a true edge for slicing and shaping. After a few days of use, the anonymous bits of wood seemed to fit our hands like cherished old tools, and we were not amused when somebody's favorite dog tried to make off with a favorite stick.

The sand we worked with varied from one site to another, but as long as it was damp and free of seaweed, shells, and pebbles, it performed admirably. Damp sand will stand at a much steeper angle than dry, and it even can be made to hold a vertical surface or slight overhang without collapsing. At about fifteen feet from the water's edge, the sand was always perfect for molding — neither too soupy nor too dry — but after a day of rain we were free to build anywhere and our shapes held beautifully.

Water is the mortar that holds our structures together. After a short exposure to the sun, the surfaces will look dry, but the sand inside remains moist for hours. Careful packing of the surfaces not only gives the objects a finished, solid look, but prevents evaporation of the vital moisture.

We soon learned that the ultimate success of a structure depended on the care we took to get our corners sharp and true and our surfaces smooth and compact. Without that care, the buildings looked unconvincing, more like crumble cookies than impressive tombs and temples. But a real master work was admired by everyone who passed. Half the fun was moving off down the beach and watching our pieces attract and astound.

The only rules needed in order to build any structure in this book are:

1) PILE
2) PACK
3) CUT

That's it. That's all there is to it!

My grandson, Sam Mott, is an eager sandbuilder. And I must admit that he's no slouch at wrecking the structures, too, when it's time to move on.

There's no getting around it: people love pyramids. Pyramids draw people like flies. They don't just look and leave either; they watch every move. Some will ask penetrating questions such as, "Are you an Egyptian?", but it's only the kids who come right out and ask to help. And once they see how easy it is to build impressive structures they become little missionaries. In a few hours there are pyramids all up and down the beach.

2
SIMPLE STRUCTURES

Some of the structures are grand to look at but take only minutes to build, while others are modest in size and deceptively tricky to get right. Still, none of them take very long, and having pint-sized commentators on hand always makes the whole process more fun.

Here you see a ribbed, truncated cone that took all of three minutes to build (*left*). Kids don't call such things "ribbed, truncated cones." Kids are more direct. They say "lampshade."

To make a cone, start piling up the sand as much as you need according to the height you desire. After you sweep your stick around a couple of times to get the cone just right it's easy to slice off a top or a side — or even scrape steps carefully into its sloping sides.

Your first few cones may be tilted, but that's okay. They'll be interesting. You'll soon learn to sweep your straight edge around at the same angle on all sides, and people will marvel at the perfection of your geometry.

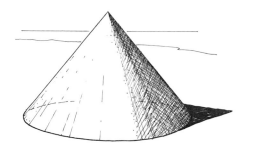

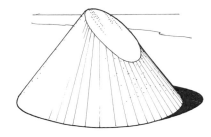

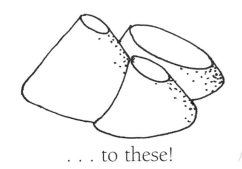

Go from this . . .   . . . to this . . .   . . . to these!

Big abstract forms (such as those on pages 84 and 87) are of course real show-stoppers on the beach — but among the smaller, simpler structures curved steps seem to be right up there with pyramids when it comes to attracting judges, commentators, helpers, wise-crackers and, now and then, young demolition experts.

. . . you find that sand itself has begun to suggest ideas, and when there is bright sunlight the forms almost leap into existence.

. . . for ideas to come along . . .

Sometimes while waiting . . .

Surprisingly, this ring-wall requires a lot of work. Well, not work, exactly, but care, because all the sand inside the wall has to be lifted out in little stickfuls or carefully pushed out through the opening.

The sundial, on the other hand, is a snap: make a flat surface, cut away the sand around it, add two pebbles and watch the earth turn. It's amazing how quickly the shadow moves across the mark.

You don't get long shadows like this during the middle of the day. Early or late sunlight is best for that . . . unless you cheat and tilt the dial.

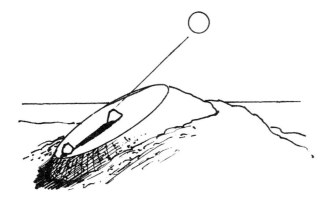

Even grizzled old beach bums — I mean professional sand artists like us — are continually amazed by some of the effects we get. Working a few feet apart, talking about the sound of the waves or the warmth of the breeze, we suddenly discover that we've created, almost without thinking, a series of curved steps that seem almost concrete-like in appearance.

And serrations! They seem to roll out by the yard, they're so easy to create. That's why you'll see a lot of them in this book: big effects from little work. You simply use your stick on the platforms you've created to texturize them.

Throughout this book you'll see nice fluffy sand all around our works. The texture doesn't occur by itself. If we didn't go back after completing each piece and throw handfuls of sand carefully around the objects, you'd see knee dents, footprints, handprints, and all the other evidences of our having worked around the pieces. The look of undisturbed sand right up to the edges of the smooth surfaces adds an extra layer of unbelievability to the discovery of these strange architectures on the summer beach.

For these serrated extravaganzas we reversed the procedure, creating a big area of fluffy sand first and then adding the radiating ribs.

These kinds of "roads" are fun to drive on if you don't mind being shaken alive. And since they're likely to lead anywhere, there's always that hope of discovering something around the next bend.

To build a house, first pile up the sand, execute six quick cuts, then fluff up the trampled surroundings. finally, press the walk and the patio into the obliging fluff using the flat surface of the stick. The magic is in the sunlight; without it there'd be almost nothing to see.

Listen to those glorious waves! Talk about inspirational background music! Here you can see how the trampled sand near the house has been made to look untouched. All it takes are a few careful sideways tosses to get the even texture.

3

FORMAL STRUCTURES

We had a wealth of building styles to draw from, stretching back five thousand years. Man's earliest buildings depended on the force of gravity, stone upon stone, more than any internal framework to keep them standing, so they're particularly well suited to reproduction in sand. Like all self-respecting architects, we borrowed ideas from different eras and far-flung continents, gaining a knowledgeable respect for our ancient colleagues along the way. We also began to view the buildings around us in a new way, almost as sculpture, noting the play of light and shadow and wondering how they would look in sand.

In the photo on the opposite page you can see all the rules in a single picture, everything from the scattered sand in the foreground to the suggestions of horizontal stone-coursing in pyramids. You also see the two key photo principles:

1) *Shoot toward the light–dark corner of the object.*
2) *Get down low so it towers above the horizon, the lower the better.*

Sun, sea, and sand.

One of our earlier efforts was the elegant Egyptian pyramid. These royal tombs were actually as tall as five hundred feet, covering thirteen acres, but our small version captured the feeling of mass and awed bathers and joggers with its mystery.

Simple shapes like this one are not the easiest to construct, but mastering these crisp corners and smooth faces gave us the skill we needed to make any other sand construction look convincing, solid, and larger than life.

NOTE:

Perhaps it's best to pause here and say a word of encouragement to all the Iowans, Denverites, and citizens of Fargo who are bursting with latent sand-talent but aren't within sound of ocean waves. After all, there's no need for saltwater, tides, and waves in the making of sandtiquities. Many of America's lakes and rivers have sandy beaches, and even the sand in an Oklahoma sandbox can be shaped into some amazing structures once a bit of moisture is added to the grains.

There's never a shortage of help when sandtiquities are in progress, and it's heartening to see how quickly kids learn to use sunlight and shadows as guides to smooth surfaces.

Notice how trampled the sand gets from all the activity. But again, a few well-tossed handfuls erase all signs of activity.

The basic pyramid is built on a square base, and marking out the square before carving the sides helped us find the right proportions. The crooked shadow tells us we sliced unevenly. The power of these structures cannot be overstated, crumbly sand though they may be.

Here we started with a simple pyramid and carved further, lopping off the top and reshaping the sides. The cuts took less than a minute, then we stood back and admired the sun's effect. The twisted, truncated pyramid strikes many observers as being almost impossible for an amateur to build. The truth, of course, is that it is amazingly simple. The four sides require just four downward slices, but instead of going straight down the slopes the straight edge is simply turned as it descends, the same amount of turn on each face.

A bird's–eye view revealed a striking pinwheel.

This stepped pyramid is based on a variety found throughout Central America. The stairs were on one or more faces and the priests would climb them to the top level where they performed human sacrifices. Our version seemed to possess a mysterious power that drew an audience from all over the beach, even though no one was taken on a one-way trip to the top.

We start with a basic pyramid, level the top, and square it. Then we inscribe the sides of the ramp, pressing in with the edges of our stick. Using the end of the stick, we push in little steps and then use the width of the stick to flatten the bands next to the steps. Also use the width of the stick to slice the big steps from the sloping sides.

We ran a ramp around this pyramid and then gave it some walls as it meandered along the beach. We watched the shadows in all the work we did. They showed every flaw and kept our carving regular and smooth. Sometimes, once the surfaces were smooth and flat and the corners sharp, we gave our pyramids added authenticity and scale by pushing faint horizontal dents into the faces. It looks as if they were built up of great dressed stones when done right. Practice gave us a lighter touch — the slightest indentation catches the light when surfaces are even.

The things that take us just a few minutes to accomplish took years when every stone had to be cut by hand, halved into place, and set exactly to the lines established by the mathematicians. From Egypt to Peru giant blocks of stone weighing many tons were cut and then somehow fitted so carefully together that even today it is impossible to slip even a slender knife blade into their joints.

Our sandtiquities help to carry us back over the centuries to a greater appreciation of what has gone before, and we suddenly realize that even then children were probably creating structures much like ours, using as their models the giant stone edifices slowly rising from the plains.

The ziggurat was like an artificial mountain built high above the plains to support a sacred shrine. The shrine, reaching up to the heavens, was meant to attract a visitation of a deity. Ruins of more than thirty ziggurats still exist in the Middle East. Our version is modeled after the ruins at Ur, and, to the best of our knowledge, it attracted no gods but many, many pilgrims in bathing suits.

We didn't finish this building in the usual smooth, even way because it looked like a creditable ruin in its rough state. The condition of the sand reminded us of ancient bricks, so we took it one step further and experimented with a texture on the walls.

A ziggurat, an ancient Persian temple on a man-made hill.

Methuselah at work.

Local color.

When we began this structure it was only a stepped round thing, but our spectators and critics insisted it was a Greek amphitheater, and who were we to argue? We didn't faithfully follow the ancient design but tried to imagine tiny actors and spectators in scale and finished our theater to that purpose.

It didn't take long to discover that, unlike most buildings, which are built starting from the lowest level, an amphitheater done in sand must be built starting at the top. Cutting each step with careful slow curving sweeps produces so much fallen debris there's no other way to work than from the top.

At right you see the amphitheater with its gateway as well as the carefully flung cover-up sand, but perhaps you haven't yet noticed how the steps become a solid-looking mound when you turn the picture upside down.

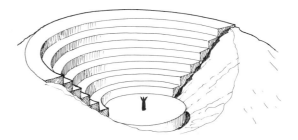

These barrel-vaulted dwellings are modeled after a type that originated in ancient Greece, and it was easy to imagine them serenely facing the Aegean Sea. Traditionally, each little loaf was a single room and there were no interior connections between them. Since ours was built on a steep hillside, we made it a split-level, and we improvised with windows and ridges along the roofs. After all, we are architects, not drudges. There's little visible here to suggest the great difficulty of making the 4-way vaults compared with the utter one-minute simplicity of making those single arches. It's carving the intersections that's the challenge.

The loaves of the houses were built one at a time, no preplanning necessary. After each was shaped, we pushed more sand up to it and built another, then leveled the site. (As the family grows so does the number of rooms!)

We added the dome to the flattened roof and shaped it firmly before slicing away the walls. The entrance gives a touch of realism and scale. Sharp angles and planes of light and shadow gave our little house substance. A desert family could move right in.

There was a lot of satisfaction in building smaller structures. They had a different but powerful appeal, perhaps because their scale was immediately apparent. Our ever-changing audience seemed to think that gnomes lived in them. One young fellow even tried to peer through the doorway.

Domed houses like this one were built in the Middle East centuries ago. They had thick, windowless walls and inset doorways to keep out the fierce desert heat.

As seen on the opposite page, the caravanserai were desert inns found everywhere in the Middle East, often spaced a day's journey apart. The domed roofs gave an inkling of what the interior space would be like, a dark and airy haven in the scorching desert. This is only one of many roof forms that man has drawn from nature.

We roughly cut the walls from a heap of sand and formed the top into irregular domes, supporting the wall with one hand. We quickly learned how hard we could pat without causing a collapse. A small mound of sand added to the front wall was cut into buttresses. (OPPOSITE)

4

COMPLEXES

The practice of burrowing into cliffs and walls was common all over the ancient world. Our adaptation was based on the Anatolian hill villages, where conical volcanic formations were eroded by wind and weather and the natural caves were carved out further by the ancients and used as dwellings. We should admit that our little hills did not occur volcanically on the beach — we heaped and packed them.

The only problem with natural-looking structures is that they're so unnoticeable; people walk right over them without ever seeing them. But rather than turn loose the savage animals we keep chained in the caves, we just shook our heads and smiled remembering how many Anatolian towns we've also inadvertently stepped on.

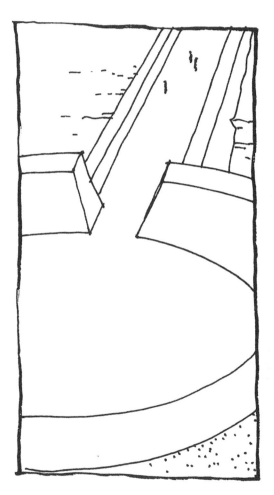

Very often the tides will help by creating little two- or three-foot-high cliffs on parts of the beach. With all that work done for us we can go crazy carving out levels and steps and caves that sometimes run for twenty or thirty feet along the "cliffs." It's hard work, but somebody's got to do it.

Rough textures, too, are achieved with the straight edge. Doorways are poked in with a handy barrette. All that's missing is the rope ladder.

Our walled city was really just a rough sketch of a town, an impression built of many details. The varying height of the wall and of the buildings within suggested a natural topography of the land. Steps and stairways were suggested to connect the levels. Often all that remained of the real walled cities were the massive retaining walls. Here, the wall not only makes our town invincible, but gives it a satisfying unity. It is entirely self-contained, a democratic city-state, we like to think.

The wall is first cut and formed around a shapeless mound. Then we stamped out the town with a new tool, a small square block nailed to a straight edge. We pressed lightly for a roof top, harder for a courtyard, twirled it for circles, angled it, and made steps with it. And just when we needed a bit of human scale along came a woman who lent us her feet to be immortalized forever.

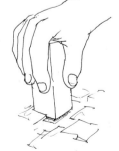

Our forts are havens in the rugged wilderness. We're on the defensive here, secure against any enemy attack — except the dreaded beach ball. The interior ramp and the textures are the kinds of details that give scale to any construction and add to the illusion. Just remember to allow an additional twenty minutes for the excavating of sand from the interior courtyards. Most of it can be scooped out in a hurry, but when you get down to the final floor level many tiny loads must be removed before all signs of construction disappear.

This gateway ended up looking surprisingly solid. The mound we started from was quite rough, but notice the evenness and sharp detail on the part we have formed. How many soldiers could march abreast through this gate?

Pile, pack, and cut.

As beginners we were obsessed with the size and scope of single structures, but we soon discovered the thrill of ranging over wide areas, transforming the landscape with our works. We let the existing contours of the beach influence us in designing the spaces between our structures and left natural areas to contrast with our carved planes and shapes. As we created, we tried to imagine the flow of activities that might take place on our landscapes — in miniature, of course!

We like to combine simple shapes, loosely based on ancient ones, in brand new ways, with only inspiration to guide us. Sometimes we find we are more interested in these combinations than in structures.

We take the natural slope of the beach, define it with smooth planes, and add some mysterious structures. They're not hard to see when viewed from the shady side like this but from the other direction all you see, unless you look closely, is a lot of sand; consequently herds of beach people sometimes walk right through. When they do we always hope they won't notice what they've done. Their embarrassment on realizing it is too painful to watch. Repairing the damage is easy, and it often leads to designs suggested by the damage.

5

MONUMENTS

Monuments of kings and gods always convey messages of power. The approach is usually long and arduous, and once inside, you feel dwarfed. It's not an accident or casual choice that many banks look like Greek temples.

It's hard for sand to stand up in front of you in this way when all it wants to do is lie on the beach, but to tell you the truth I think it does like to show off a bit. For thousands of years all it has done is let the winds and the tides push it around. Now it has something to show its grandchildren: "Look, I'm a Greek temple."

Well, there was just time enough to rough up the sand around the steps, scrunch way down in the sand, and take the pictures before the drying wind began to nibble at the corners, showing the grains who was boss.

Once again, sunlight saved the day. Notice how you tend to believe the light and shade solidity of the form rather than the all-too-obvious crumbliness of the little sand temple? Has the great tourist attraction of Athens appeared on a Cape Cod beach before? Probably not. You may consider this a first.

High up in the Andes are the ruins of Machu Picchu, a sort of vast theater-in-the-round that held as many as sixty thousand people. We can only guess at the spectacles that took place there and marvel at the engineering skill of the ancient Incas. The actual tiers are each six feet high and twenty-three feet deep, carved right out of the mountain. These were monumental works, and our little sand model captured their scale admirably. Now turn the pictures upside down and see what happens.

Even with the ocean in the background it's hard to tell the size of our Machu Picchu. Judge by the carving tool — it's that small!

Special rules for creating a Sphinx: pile, pack, cut. Cut down the sides of the head and ears, then the body, then the legs. Sometimes parts will collapse but replacement is easy.

A first look at our Sphinx made us wonder if our simple attempt would ever impress anyone, but when the light was right, we flopped down on our bellies and thought it looked rather profound. "It's exactly like a real sphinx," our audience said. We didn't give them an argument.

The Buddha figure is formed with the usual straight edge, but it's used with a rolling motion of the flat side, cutting, packing, and shaping at the same time. The fleshy, almost obscene lump manages to convince us of its serenity as it sits in a place of honor.

This was a fifteen-minute project, a race against the tide, which was lapping at our steps. Then we let the ocean wash the great Buddha away.

"What do you mean, you 'let it'? Did you have any choice in the matter?"

No.

Wasn't it a team of Swedish engineers who managed to save this immense cliff sculpture from the waters rising behind Egypt's Aswan Dam? Not only did the piece have to be cut loose from its surrounding bedrock, it then had to be jacked up the cliff with the utmost care.

Well, almost. This is not the actual Abu Simbel in these pictures. We tricked you; this is just a little twelve-inch sand sculpture.

For our version of the Great Wall of China, we made a mound that snaked along the beach following miniature hills and valleys. We added turrets of our own design and other little effects.

Obviously, almost anything goes when you're building a wall like this. Turrets and gateways conceal awkward intersections of planes. The main characteristic is the zig-zaggy rambliness as the ancient wall winds its way over hills and valleys.

Our beach cliff was only three or four feet high but the angle tricks the eye.

How far is it from China to Tibet? About twenty feet where we come from. Some of the same repose you see in the Great Wall is apparent here: walls that are battered (sloped backward against the mountain for stability), simplicity, and a unity of design that carries through the entire structure.

Sand acts in some ways very much like stone. When it's massed and sloped this way it is quite stable. This cliffside complex remained for several days on the beach, a far cry from our almost instantly crumbling Parthenon with its unstable forced verticals.

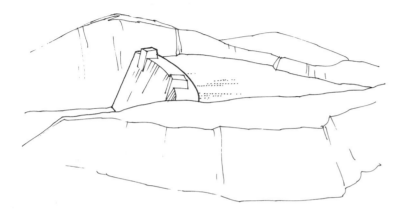

We arrived at the beach one day full of enough energy and ambition to move the earth. We constructed this dam instead. It's another sort of monumental design that gained its credibility through our molding of the ravines and valley behind it, and the great basin that suggested a vast upriver reservoir. The afternoon sun lent a dramatic effect and convinced us of our dam's solidity. Talk about a show-stopper!

The vertical face of the dam was packed tightly and smoothly to give it a man-made look to contrast with the rougher surroundings. The water level was carefully graded. The dam's top wall was built up by packing a small mound of damp sand on the top of the edge of the arc and carving it into a raised rim. The two watch towers were also built from a small heap of sand and then packed and cut away.

LAY OF THE LAND

Along the beach you will find all sorts of mounds and tidal benches and strange configurations — sometimes the remnants of the play of others — which make splendid springboards for a little carving and readapting of your own.

Pile, pack, and cut, starting, of course, at the top, cleaning and perfecting each level before moving down to the one below. Once a design system like this is under way it's easy to carry it forward. And then suddenly a variation will occur and off you go!

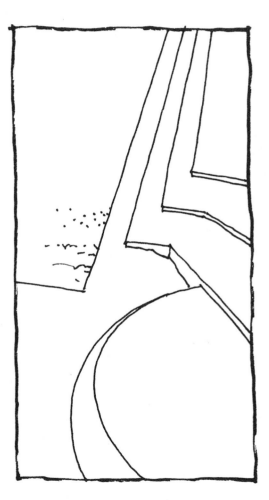

Here we had little height so we played with the angles instead. Sometimes we placed angle on angle.

Another way we connected structures and created complexes was by curving out steps and terraces. These differ from formal bases and plazas mostly in their abstract designs. Often, a base became a plaza when it stretched out before a building or monument, and steps grew broader and broader until they were terraces. They all tended to flow together and follow the lay of the beach when inspiration was upon us. When we were done, the eye played tricks, picking out what seemed to be a foot-sized step and enlarging everything around that accordingly. Are these steps a person would walk up, or sit on, or climb?

Whatever scale we chose to work in, the effects we achieved were well beyond the actual size of our creations. It was always a surprise to smooth off a vast plain, lay our stick aside, sink down on the sand and gaze up at the sweeping landscape we created.

Then came the day when we didn't feel geometrical at all and our terraces undulated along the sloping sand with no plan other than our own amusement and satisfaction.

These abstract fancies, too, drew the attention of every passerby. What could be more appropriate than waves on the beach? Groundworks can cover a lot of area in a very short time and sharpen up your carving and packing skills. It gives a feeling of real power to transform a strip of beach this way.

You have to take your life in your hands sometimes, working on these dizzying heights, but somebody's got to do it, and it's important that those matchstick people keep moving along that narrow trail. Notice how the cliffs have broken away in great crystalline planes over the centuries, creating the piled rubble at the base.

This inspiring heap was found at the base of a lifeguard's chair. We went to work with our straight edges and turned it into a primitive mountainside village, making it up as we went along. By the time we were through, it was covered with dwellings and storehouses, shrines, corridors, and steps in every direction. There were terraces all down the front, and most of the windows and doorways faced out to sea.

The sand wall shown here had some vertical grooves. We packed it tighter and carved a very shallow cave and more vertical and horizontal details and had a perfect spot for a Pueblo village.

Mesas and buttes are the remains of what was once a flat plain, level with their tops. Then, over immense periods of time, the actions of wind, water and freezing eroded most of the land away, leaving only the hardest parts of the rock standing. If you've been to the Southwest you've seen the magnificent results. Your results may not be as magnificent, but you'll be amazed by what you can create.

Remember Devil's Tower from Close Encounters of the Third Kind? *We thought we might lure a tiny UFO with this replica. It took only a few minutes to shape the tower top, rocking the edge of our stick against it to give it texture.*

We started with a simple heap of sand, sculpted the ridge, flattened it and then added tiny cliff faces. If you put your chin in the sand and looked to the sky, it became a mesa!

Greetings, Earthlings!

The rectangular forms of these Pueblo dwellings were suggested by the shapes of the sun dried bricks, or adobes, made from the soil itself. The thick walls of a real adobe, permitting only slow passage of heat, kept the occupants cool in the daytime and warm at night.

Again, with your chin in the sand, and the low-angle light of dawn or of day's end, they tend to look full scale.

These circular enclosures, or "kivas," were used by the Anasazi, or "unknown ones," for secret religious ceremonies.

You can use almost anything for making the little ladder. On Cape Cod, tall grasses roll up into stiff little tubes when they're cut, ideal in size for making ladder models. A bit of white glue, a few minutes for it to dry, and violà!

7

ABSTRACTS

Turn yourself loose with a beach stick and pretty soon it can seem as if acres of foot-trampled sand have been turned into sweeping curves, black holes, or skin-smooth surfaces. Or, sometimes the surfaces are textured, but the flow is the thing — the sweep from one design to the next without any jarring breaks in the rhythm. This seems to be the most natural way to sculpt sand, but most of us, long before we get to the beach, are taught to make things: actual recognizable objects, so we lose some of our natural responsiveness to the world. Now you have a chance to find it.

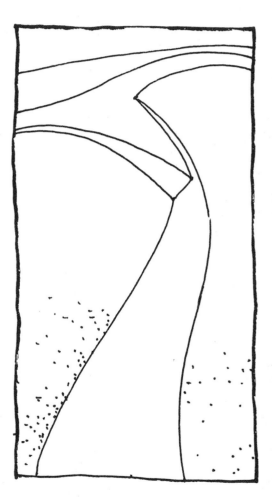

In spite of not always producing geometrical forms, most of our flights of fancy received crisp edges. This shell-like formation seems to rise in gentle curves and then becomes subterranean. The looping lines repeat the shell motif, and it emerges looking like the twisted waves of a riptide, or possibly a congregation of mollusks. One thing about abstractions, you can read almost anything into them.

The slim necklace of light above had to be photographed in a hurry, for the shadow of the dome didn't stand still. The flat plane on which the shadow fell was quickly cut away to within a fraction of an inch of the shadow's edge.

Ah, shadows! Nowhere are they more effective, more revealing, than they are on these sandy creations where anything goes.

From the excavated ram's horn motif at left to the rock-worshipping pit across the page — any of a million variations endlessly come to mind. The purpose of this book is not to show off what we've done, for anyone with a flat stick can do most of these things very easily. The purpose is rather to suggest to you the numberless possibilities that lie on the beach, and by extension the even *more* infinite numbers of possibilities that surround each of us, everywhere.

Now that you're something of an old hand at the sandtiquities business you can no doubt tell at a glance that this little job took only about five minutes. *(Cut and level the upper floor, cut and level the lower, add rock to taste.)*

8

END OF THE DAY

Nothing we built was beyond the reach of wind or tide, nor was it meant to be. It was exciting to watch an especially powerful wave crash down upon a temple or village and wipe it out, while the slower erosion of the wind set us to daydreaming. The structures fall to ruin on a tiny scale, much the way ancient stones and bricks crumbled over the course of centuries. The speeded-up natural weathering often makes a structure more impressive than it was in its first pristine minutes of completion.

The surf approaches our pyramid complex.

We came to welcome the gentle aging effects of the wind and the minor avalanches that made ruins of our work, just as the elements had created the ruins that inspired us. It was as if time had shrunk along with physical dimension, and we watched like lazy gods as the sun went down.

The next day we returned and found the previous evening's activities detailed across our work — dog tracks, bird and human footprints — but still there was a measure of respect. One doesn't lightly destroy a temple.

Now the pyramid is assaulted.

Aerial inspectors arrive to leave their calling cards.

Young boys love to do demolition work, and it's never more fun than it is on the beach where the consequences are slight.

"Thus," said Henry Thoreau, "all work passes out of the hands of the architect into the hands of nature, to be perfected."